Food-Drying T

Carol Costenbader

CONTENTS

Drying Food

Drying was one of the earliest methods of preservation humans found to save food from times of bounty to use when food was scarce. As far back as pre-biblical times, fishermen dried and smoked fish, and farmers dried olives and dates in the hot, dry climate of the Middle East.

Drying is by far the simplest and most natural way of preserving food. Little in the way of equipment is needed, but climate is every-thing. If you are fortunate enough to live in a warm, dry region, all you need is fresh food and a little time. The faster food can dry with-out actually cooking, the better its flavor will be when it's reconstituted. If you live in a relatively moist climate, you will want to learn to use a more active drying method — a dehydrator, your oven, or in some cases the sun. As always, the finished product will be only as good as the original, so start with the very best fresh food.

The concept of drying food is quite simple. When all the moisture is removed from the food, the growth of organisms that spoil food is stopped. Bacteria, mold, and yeasts can be supported only in an environment that has adequate water for them to grow. Properly dried fruits have about 80 percent of the water removed, and prop-erly dried vegetables have about 90 percent of the water removed. Thus you can count on keeping your home-dried foods for six months to two years, depending on the storage temperature (see chart on pages 18–19). Remember that cooler storage temperatures are better. Food kept at 70°F does not keep as long as food stored at 52°F.

Food Preparation for Drying

Use only blemish-free fruits and vegetables. Fruit should be fully ripe but not overly ripe. (Save overly ripe fruit for sauces or for making fruit leathers; see pages 11–12.) The smaller the piece of food to dry, the less time it will take to dry properly. Try to keep all the pieces about the same size, so each piece will dry at the same rate.

Blanching

Proper blanching, which heats the food without actually cooking it, deactivates the enzymes that cause food spoilage. For use in the drying process, steam-blanching is the only method recommended for vegetables.

The method of dipping produce in boiling water, used in many areas of the world, is not recommended because it adds more water to the produce and therefore increases drying time. Because the food is heated longer and at a hotter temperature, it also robs the food of nutrients and does not fully protect the produce from spoilage organisms. If you must boil fruits and vegetables, use about 3 gallons of water to every 1 quart of food, drain and chill the pieces in ice water to stop the cooking and then pat dry.

To steam-blanch, place produce in a steamer basket in a pan over at least 2 inches of water.

To cool, pour produce into an ice-water bath. When cool, transfer to a towel to dry.

To blanch using the steam method, you'll need a steamer, a large Dutch oven, or your canner with lid. Use a wire basket with legs, a basket that fits in the top of the pot, or a colander that will allow 2 or more inches of water to boil without touching the produce. Steam 1 minute longer than the time given if you live 5,000 feet or more above sea level (see chart on pages 18–19 for steaming times). After blanching, drain the food, then chill in ice water to stop the cooking. Drain again and dry on towels.

Blanching can be done in a microwave oven, but only in small quantities. Wattages vary, so consult the manufacturer's instructions.

DIPPING

Dip	Method	Time
Ascorbic Acid All fruits	2 Tbsp. ascorbic acid or 5 1-g crushed vitamin C tabs and 1 quart water	Dip for 5 minutes, drain well, pat dry
Honey Bananas Peaches Pineapple	3 cups water, 1 cup sugar: Heat, then add 1 cup honey; stir well	In batches, dip and remove immediately, drain well, and pat dry
Juices Apples Bananas Peaches	1 quart pineapple juice, 1 quart lukewarm water, ¼ cup bottled lemon juice	Dip no more than 10 minutes, drain well, pat dry
Pectin Berries Cherries Peaches	1 box powdered pectin, 1 cup water: Boil together 1 minute, add ½ cup sugar, cold water to make 2 cups	Glaze fruit slices with thin coating, drain well, pat dry
Salt All fruits	6 Tbsp. pickling salt, 1 gallon water	Soak no more than 5 minutes, drain, and pat dry

Other Preparations for Drying

To improve the chances for good color retention, dip the fruit slices in a prepared solution (see dipping chart on page 4). This is only partially effective, however. Steam-blanching for both fruits and vegetables is still the best way.

For decades, many people used sulfur to pretreat dried fruits to preserve color. Fruit pretreated with sulfur must be dried by the sun method. Sulfuring of fruits is not a good practice for use with a home dehydrator.

While sulfuring preserves the color and vitamin C of many fruits, it may cause allergies or asthma. Sulfur is now banned as a preservative for produce in supermarkets and in restaurant salad bars.

Four Types of Drying

Drying meat and produce involves the simple process of exposing the food to mild heat and moving air. This can be done by placing food in the sun, in a dehydrator, in the open air, or in an oven.

Air-Drying

The process of air-drying is very similar to sun-drying. Puffs of dry air circulate around the food, absorb the moisture, and carry it away. Keep the food out of direct sun to prevent loss of color.

Try air-drying steam-blanched green beans by stringing them on a cotton thread and hanging them under the eaves of the house or porch or in a well-ventilated attic. Depending on the conditions, in two or three days you will have dried, pliable "leather britches,"

To dry mushrooms, first thread them onto a clean string.

great for adding to soups. Bring the beans inside at night to prevent dew from collecting on them. Keep them out of direst sun: It will make them lose all color.

To dry mushrooms, wipe them clean, string using a needle and thread, and hang in an airy location. Or you can place clean mushrooms on several thicknesses of newspaper; turn them several times as the day progresses, and change the newspapers as moisture is absorbed. Place the mushrooms in a dry, airy spot (in direct sun if you wish, but don't forget to bring them in at night.) In one or two days the mushrooms will be almost brittle.

After the drying process, both the green beans and the mushrooms must be heated in a 175°F oven for 30 minutes to destroy insect eggs. Condition the produce (see Post-Drying Methods, page 9) and then store in a cool, dry place for up to six months.

Sun-Drying

Because sun-drying takes more time, pretreating the produce by blanching or another method is much more important. The ideal temperature is about 100°F with low humidity. If you are blessed with a climate like that, do try sun-drying. In other climates, use caution. Low temperature and high humidity is the perfect combination for spoilage to occur before drying can be accomplished.

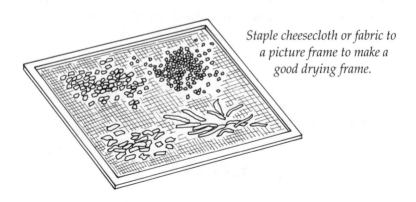

Staple cheesecloth or fabric to a picture frame to make a good drying frame.

Sun-Drying Equipment. To make sun-drying equipment, I like to use old picture frames purchased from flea markets. First, clean the frames with a cloth dampened with soap and water. Then seal the frames with mineral oil. Stretch a clean, 100 percent cotton sheet or cheesecloth over a frame and secure with a stapler. Some people use screens from their windows. This is fine, but don't use a screen with galvanized wire as it can impart off-flavors to the food. Arrange the prepared produce on the cloth, then place the frames in direct sun, bracing them so that air can circulate on all sides. (Bring them in at night to prevent dew from collecting on them.) You can turn the produce over halfway through the drying process (after about two days). In about two to four days you will have leathery but pliable produce. This is great for sun-dried tomatoes.

To destroy any pest eggs that may still be in your homegrown foods, remove the produce from the frames and freeze it for two to four days below zero or heat it in a tray in your oven 10 to 15 minutes at 175°F (see Post-Drying Methods, page 9). Whether you freeze or heat the produce, bring it to room temperature and then store in airtight jars for up to six months.

You can either purchase a commercial dehydrator or make your own.

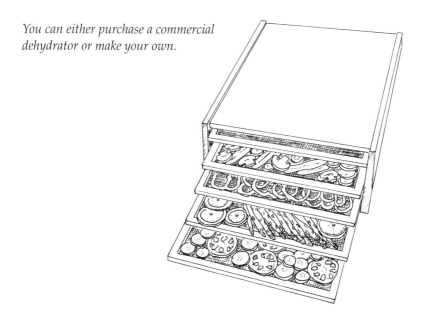

Dehydrator

Using a food dehydrator is simple: You fill the trays with prepared produce, set the timer, turn on the dehydrator, and go about your business. Although a commercial dehydrator can be expensive, it will pay for itself over several seasons. Comparison shopping is difficult, since most commercial dehydrators are sold through mail order. Plan on writing for information before ordering. Many of these companies also have Web sites on the Internet that can be accessed by searching "dehydrator" or "food drying." There are several features to consider before you buy:

- Underwriters Laboratories (UL) should approve the dehydrator for safety.
- Be sure you order a size that you can easily accommodate in your house and that will allow you to dry the right amount of produce or meat at a time.
- Trays should be lightweight and sturdy. Plastic screens are easier to clean and are better than metal. Metal screens can corrode, retain the heat longer, and may scorch food.
- If your model has a door, make sure that it opens easily and can be completely removed.
- The controls should be easy to read. Control settings to adjust vents for airflow and to regulate the heat are important, and an automatic built-in timer is useful.
- The materials used in the outside cabinets vary greatly. Consider how easily you can move the cabinet, clean it, and store it. Look for double-walled insulation, also.
- Look for dehydrators that use less electricity.

Oven-Drying

The most labor intensive of all the methods, oven drying is an effective (although possibly more expensive) process. In this method, place the food directly on oven racks or cover the racks with clean, 100 percent cotton sheeting or cheesecloth.

Preheat your oven to 145°F. Check the temperature periodically with an oven thermometer. Ovens vary, so you may need to experiment with a setting between 120°F and 145°F. My gas oven dries produce best at 145°F. Use a wooden spoon to prop open the door to let the moisture escape. Be sure not to have your oven too full, or the drying time will become quite long. Allow 4 to 12 hours, depending on the items and quantities being dried. Food should be dry but pliable when cool. (Test one or two pieces.)

While some authorities claim that it's possible to dry food in a microwave oven, I don't recommend it, because the microwave will cook your produce before it dries. However, you can easily dry herbs in the microwave with good results.

Post-Drying Methods

After the food is dried, condition it by pouring it into a large open container such as a big enameled canner pot. Don't use a container that is aluminum or that is porous, because it might affect the flavor or consistency of the dried food. Put the pot in a warm but dry and airy place. For the next 10 days or two weeks, stir it once or twice a day. Don't add newly dried food to the batch in the pot, as you want it all to finish drying at the same time.

Pasteurizing

Pasteurizing is the partial sterilization of food. Because outdoor drying and oven-drying are less exact, pasteurizing dried food is recommended.

Squeeze excess air from storage bags and then pack them in brown paper bags to protect produce from light.

The longer you wish to keep the dried food, the more the need for pasteurizing increases. Pasteurizing ensures that insect eggs and organisms that cause spoilage are destroyed, allowing food to be stored for a longer period.

There are two ways to pasteurize:

- **Heat.** Spread the dried produce on trays in a thin layer and leave in your 175°F oven for 10 to 15 minutes. Cool.
- **Freeze.** Using plastic storage bags, place dried produce in a zero-degree freezer two to four days. This destroys fewer vitamins than does the oven method. The freezer must be at zero. The freezer compartment of a refrigerator will not do.

Packing and Storing

Dried food should be packed promptly in a "user-friendly" quantity ready for your meal preparation. As light, moisture, and air are hard on dried foods, a cool, dry, dark place is best. (This does not necessarily mean the refrigerator, which is moist and dark.) Completely fill a clean, airtight glass container or a clean zip-sealed bag with all the air squeezed out. Put the jars or plastic bags inside a brown paper grocery bag to protect them from the light. Label the dried foods carefully, being certain to date them properly. Always use the oldest package first. If summer's heat becomes a problem, switch to the refrigerator, but make certain the packaging is absolutely airtight to guard against moisture.

Rehydrating

To rehydrate dried produce, first cover it with boiling water. Let the produce stand for several hours to absorb the water, then cook the produce in the soaking liquid that is left. Vegetables take longer to rehydrate than fruits because they lose more water to dehydration. Cooking time will be much shorter than for produce not rehydrated before cooking. In the case of dried beans, drain the rehydrated beans and cook them in fresh water, because the nitrogen released by the beans in the soaking water is difficult to digest. Cook until tender.

Fruit Leathers

Apples, bananas, peaches, and berries are perfect for fruit leathers. Many adventurous people enjoy vegetable leathers as well. But the children's favorite, "fruit rolls" or "fruit taffy," as leathers are often called, has an incredible amount of concentrated natural sugar that frequently sticks to teeth. For that reason, health professionals suggest that the teeth be cleaned soon after you eat this tasty treat. Leathers from cooked fruits will be very vibrant in color.

Puree

The first step in making fruit leathers is to pare and pit carefully washed, ripe raw fruit and process it through a food mill. I like the Squeezo Strainer and the Victorio Strainer because they separate the small seeds and skins and leave you with a thick, rich puree. A blender or food processor can also be used for this. It may be necessary to add a small amount of liquid (juice or water will do) to reach pouring consistency. There's no need to strain fruit if a blender or processor is used. However, this is a matter of personal choice.

Another pureeing method, is to simmer clean, pared, and pitted fruit in a little water or juice for 10 to 15 minutes or until the mixture is broken down. Make sure you've added enough liquid to prevent it from burning. Then process in your food mill as described above.

If you are using a food dehydrator to make fruit leathers, follow the manufacturer's directions.

Food mills help you puree fruits for leathers.

Oven-Drying Fruit Leathers

To dehydrate your puree in the oven, use 10½ x 15½-inch standard cookie sheets with sides. Line each cookie sheet with plastic wrap or freezer paper, then pour 2 to 2¼ cups of puree onto each one. You'll want the puree to be ⅛ to ¼ inch thick. Place the cookie sheets in a 120°F oven for 12 to 16 hours. Use an oven thermometer and set the door ajar with a wooden spoon handle to maintain low heat and let the moisture escape. When the leather easily pulls away from the wrap, after 6 to 8 hours, turn over the leather onto another prepared sheet, peel off the old wrap, and continue drying in the oven for another 6 to 8 hours.

When it's done, remove the wrap and allow the leather to cool for several hours on a cake rack. Dust with cornstarch before rolling to prevent sticking. Roll the leather into a flute shape. Some people like to stack layers — to do this, cornstarch dusting is a must. Store in an airtight container.

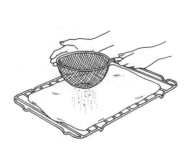

Drying Herbs

Dried herbs have been used since ancient times as medicines to remedy common ailments, to mask the taste of rancid food, and to elevate the simplest dish to a masterpiece. They enhance almost any part of the meal and can be used in all kinds of foods, even desserts. With health-conscious people looking for ways to perk up flavor without using salt or fat, herbs have now come into their own.

New research has come out to back up traditional knowledge, suggesting that many herbs may be useful in treating physical and mental maladies. While the Food and Drug Administration prohibits manufacturers from making unsubstantiated medical claims, more people are looking to herbs as a natural alternative to prescription medicine. Herbs are also being used more frequently for cosmetic purposes.

But by far the most common use of herbs is in the kitchen. With many herbs so easy to grow, whether in a kitchen garden or on a windowsill, cooks are relying on them to add zest to their fare.

Preserving herbs and using them in combination with other foods makes sense, and

Best Herbs for Drying

Bay leaf	Mint
Caraway seed	Mustard seed
Chamomile	Oregano
Dill seed	Rosemary
Lavender	Sage
Lemon peel	Savory
Lovage	Scented geranium
Marjoram	Thyme

Cut herbs to within about 6 inches of the base of the plant to hang-dry.

the process of preserving herbs by drying is simple. While they do not exactly impart the same flavor as fresh herbs, dried herbs are a staple on any kitchen shelf and can be relied on to add spark to the taste of almost any dish.

Be careful substituting dried herbs in a recipe that calls for fresh herbs. A rule of thumb is that 1 teaspoon of chopped fresh herbs is equivalent to ¼ teaspoon of powdered herbs, or ½ teaspoon of crushed dried herbs. Adjust the amounts in your recipes accordingly.

Harvesting and Air-Drying Herbs

Herbs should be harvested when their essential oils are at the highest level, usually right before flowering or bolting time (when they form seeds). The best time of the day to harvest them is before the hot sun wilts them but after the dew has evaporated. Cut them within 6 to 8 inches of the base of the plant. Some herbalists recommend not washing the leaves unless they are filled with grit or beaten down from rain, as washing depletes some of their essence. You might try hosing the plants the night before you plan to pick

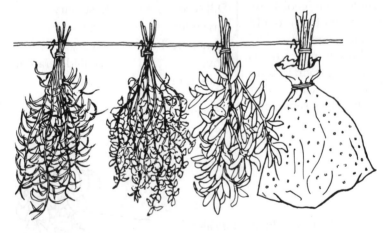

Hang herbs upside down on a wire, string, or drying rack to dry. If dust will be a problem, dry them inside small paper bags with holes or slits for air circulation.

them. Give them a good shake and make certain they are upright and not weighted down with water. The next day they will be grit-free and won't require washing after harvesting.

To dry the cut herbs, tie together small bunches of them with garden twine and hang them with leaves pointed downward in an airy, warm, dry place that's not in direct sunlight. Gravity will force the essential oils downward into the leaves.

Never hang herbs over the stove, refrigerator, or freezer. Heat from these appliances causes deterioration. Also, don't store your purchased herbs and spices in cabinets above these appliances.

If you plan to use a dehydrator, consult the manufacturer's directions for drying herbs.

Before storing, test for remaining moisture. Put dried herbs, stems and all, in airtight containers in a warm place for a day or two. If there is moisture present on the inside of the container, it is better to take the herbs back to the drying process. When the herb leaves are completely dry, put them on a tray and into a warm oven for 2 to 3 minutes to further dry them. Remove the leaves from the stem by stripping them off. Store the leaves, undisturbed, in a cool place with no direct sun, ideally in a dark glass container and/or inside a kitchen cabinet. Crush the leaves between your hands for cooking as needed: The crushing releases the pungent flavors and aroma. A mortar and pestle can be used to grind the leaves into powder. Either way, deterioration sets in within six months to a year, so plan on starting over with new batches the next season.

Oven-Dried Herbs

Start with herbs that are clean and if washed, have been patted dry. Use a cookie sheet to spread the herbs in a single layer. Set the oven to 140°F and heat the herbs in a single layer. (This will not be exact, much the way heating a room with a woodstove is not exact.) To allow the moisture to escape, prop the oven door ajar with a wooden spoon handle. Keep the temperature even by not opening the door farther to peek in too often. Better yet, use an oven ther-mometer to help you regulate the temperature. After 45 minutes, remove herbs from the oven. Let them cool and then stand for about 12 hours or overnight.

To check for moisture, try the prestorage method of enclosing the dried, cooked herbs in a glass jar for 24 hours. If moisture appears on the inside of the glass, return the herbs to the oven briefly. When they are completely dry, store them in a cool, dark place in an airtight container.

Drying Herbs in the Microwave

Microwaved herbs are labor intensive but the drying takes less time overall. All the herbs and seeds mentioned on page 13 can be dried this way. Make sure you start with clean herbs. If necessary, rinse well and pat dry with a paper towel. Use just leaves from the stems or pinch off small clusters of leaves to dry. There is no need to waste energy and time microwaving the stems, especially since they are thicker and would take longer to dry than the leaves. Work in small batches.

First, layer several thicknesses of paper towels in the microwave, and then spread the leaves or clusters in a single layer. Heat on high 1 or 2 minutes, depending on your oven. Then rotate the towels 180 degrees and repeat the 1- or 2-minute heating. Times will vary for different ovens and herbs. By the end of the second microwave time you should have noticeably drier leaves. Be careful here; you don't want to overdo it. Continue processing for about 30 seconds at a time. To test, remove one or two leaves and let them cool completely to see if they're brittle. When they are, cool the whole batch on a wire rack and store in a dark airtight container, giving the leaves the moisture test described on page 15. If the container remains free of any moisture, you are ready to store your herbs. They should retain their flavor for six months to a year.

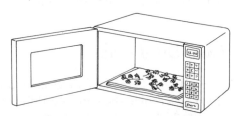

Microwave-drying is quicker and preserves more of the herbs' fresh color.

Drying Meats

Meats are dried in much the same way as fruits and vegetables, but the drying temperature must be held at 140°F to 150°F to prevent spoilage. Except when you're making meat jerky, all meats must be cooked before drying. To obtain the longest possible storage time, one year, use only the freshest lean beef and store the finished product in zip-seal bags in the freezer. Dried meats will keep for two months in the refrigerator.

Meat jerky, which can be marinated for additional flavor before drying, has a much shorter shelf life than dried meat that is cooked first. It will keep two to six months, but it is easy to prepare and very convenient to use. I store jerky in the freezer in zip-sealed bags.

Pork does not perform well because it contains more fat than lean cuts of beef and the fat can turn rancid. Chicken should not be used either; it also contains too much fat for successful drying, and may present a health hazard. As stated before, lean beef is the most reliable choice for dried meat.

Drying Beef

In a heavy saucepan, cover with water 2 pounds of lean beef cut into 1-inch cubes (lean lamb may be used); boil, covered, for about 1 hour. Spread the pieces in a single layer on trays or cookie sheets and dry them in the oven at 140°F to 150°F for 4 to 6 hours. Prop open the oven door with the handle of a wooden spoon to let the moisture escape. To test, cool a cube and cut it open to check for moisture in the center. After 4 to 6 hours, continue drying the meat but lower the temperature to 130°F; dry until there is no moisture in the center of the cubes. An oven thermometer will help you maintain a stable low temperature.

To rehydrate, use 1 cup of boiling water over 1 cup of meat. Let stand 3 to 4 hours. Use in stews, casseroles, or soups. Plan to marinate for flavor if necessary.

You can speed up the rehydration process by simmering the meat and water, in the same 1:1 ratio, in a covered saucepan for 40 to 50 minutes.

Cutting meat into small pieces aids the drying process.

DRYING VEGETABLES AND FRUITS

Best Vegetables/ Fruits for Drying	Preparation	Preferred Pretreat Method
VEGETABLES		
Beans (green, wax, yellow)	trim or shell, string to air-dry	steam-blanch 4–6 minutes
Beans (all others)	shell, pick over mature beans	steam-blanch 5 minutes
Corn	shuck, cut kernels off after blanching	steam-blanch whole 10–15 minutes
Mushrooms	wipe clean, string to air-dry or air-dry on paper	steam-blanch 3 minutes if not air drying
Okra	slice	steam-blanch 5 minutes
Peas	shell	steam-blanch 3 minutes
Peppers (chile)	string whole, air-dry	not necessary
Peppers (bell)	slice or chop	not necessary
Tomatoes, Italian	slice in half lengthwise, remove seeds, air-dry	not necessary
FRUITS		
Apples	peel, core, slice	juice or ascorbic dip, or steam-blanch 5 minutes
Apricots	slice, pit	juice or ascorbic dip, or steam-blanch 5 minutes
Bananas	peel, slice	honey, juice pectin, or ascorbic dip, or steam-blanch 5 minutes
Berries: blackberries, blueberry, cranberry	drop in boiling water to burst	honey or pectin dip
Cherries	pit	pectin, juice, or ascorbic dip
Figs	remove stem	not necessary
Grapes	remove from stem	break skin
Peaches	peel, pit, slice, or halve	honey, pectin, or juice or ascorbic dip
Pears	peel, slice, or halve	ascorbic dip, or steam-blanch 2 minutes
Plums/prunes	pit, halve, or leave whole	break skin
Strawberries	halve	honey dip

Oven or Electric Dehydrator (hrs.)	Sun/ Air (days)	Final Consistency	1 cup dry = cups cooked	Cooking time (min.)	Storage time at 52°F (months)
12–14	2–3	leathery	2½	45	8–12
48	4–5	hard	varies	120–180	8–12
8–12	1–2	dry, brittle	2	50	8–12
8–12	1–2	leathery	1¼	20–30	4–6
8–12	1–2	dry, brittle	1½	30–45	9–12
12–18	2–3	shriveled	2	40–45	8–12
not recomm.	2–3	shriveled	1½	use directly	16–24
12–18	1–2	leathery	1½	30–45	
6–8	1–2	pliable, leathery	1½	30	6–9
6–8	2–3	pliable, leathery	1¼	30	18–24
8–12	2–3	pliable, leathery	1½	30–45	24–32
6–8	2	brittle	.....	not recomm.	12–16
12–24	2–4	hard	.....	not recomm.	18–24
12–24	2–4	hard	1½	30–45	36–48
36–48	5–6	shriveled	.....	not recomm.	18–24
24–48	3–6	shriveled	.....	not recomm.	18–24
10–12	2–6	leathery	1¼	20–30	18–24
12–18	2–3	leathery	1½	20–30	18–24
12–18	4–5	shriveled	1½	20–30	24–32
8–12	1–2	hard	.....	not recomm.	18–24

Recipes

Once you've become adept at drying foods, you will want recipes that feature some of your favorite dried fruits, vegetables, and meats.

BLUEBERRY WAFFLES

Dried blueberries bring a bit of summer to a winter's brunch menu.
Substitute dried raspberries or strawberries for a delicious flavor change.

- 1¾ cups all-purpose flour
- 3 teaspoons baking powder
- ¼ teaspoons salt
- 2 eggs
- 1¼ cups milk
- 6 tablespoons vegetable oil
- 1 cup dried blueberries

1. In a medium-size bowl, combine the dry ingredients.

2. In a large mixing bowl, beat the eggs until they are light colored and foamy. Add the milk and oil. Mix and set aside.

3. Gradually add the mixed dry ingredients to the egg mixture. Beat until just smooth. Fold in the dried blueberries.

4. Pour the batter onto a hot waffle iron, following manufacturer's directions for baking.

MOCK BOURSIN HERB-CHEESE APPETIZER

Summer's dried herbs help make this mock Boursin cheese appetizer a great gift when packed in a ceramic crock with lid.

- 2 packages (8 ounces each) cream cheese, softened
- 2 teaspoons garlic powder
- 2 tablespoons milk
- 1 teaspoon dried parsley
- ¾ teaspoon salt
- ½ teaspoon dried basil leaves
- ¼ teaspoon dried tarragon
- ¼ teaspoon dried chives
- ½ teaspoon caraway seeds
- ½ teaspoon dried sage
- ¼ teaspoon dried thyme

Freshly ground black pepper
½   **cup butter, softened**

1. Combine all the ingredients in a food processor and blend until smooth.

2. Spoon into ceramic crocks or ramekins.

3. Store, well wrapped, in the refrigerator for 1 week, or freeze for up to 2 months.

HERB BUTTER BLEND

This spread makes a great herb butter with an Italian accent! If you are rushed, roll the stick of butter in the herb mixture and let guests spread it on their own bread at the table.

¼   **cup garlic powder**
¼   **cup dried minced garlic**
¼   **cup dried basil**
¼   **cup dried parsley**
1   **tablespoon paprika**
1   **teaspoon freshly ground black pepper**

1. Combine all the ingredients and store the mix in an airtight jar away from heat and light.

2. When ready to use, mix 2 tablespoons of herb mixture with 1 stick of softened butter or margarine.

3. Spread the mixture on top of or between slices of bread and warm in the oven.

HUMMUS WITH DRIED TOMATOES

This favorite dip, borrowed from the Middle East, brings a bit of summer heat when you use last year's sun-dried tomatoes and spicy red pepper flakes.

1   **can (15 ounces) chickpeas, rinsed and drained**
1   **cup sun-dried tomatoes**
2   **cloves garlic, minced**
½   **cup mayonnaise (regular or low fat)**
¼   **cup freshly grated Parmesan cheese**

1. Puree the chickpeas in the food processor. Add the tomatoes and process again. Add the garlic, mayonnaise, and cheese and process until the mixture is smooth.

2. Serve immediately with crackers, flat bread, or vegetable sticks.

3. *To freeze:* Pour hummus into a clean freezer container. Label and freeze. When you're ready to use the hummus, let it thaw in the refrigerator.

EIGHT-BEAN SALAD

For a great gift, layer the dried beans to create contrasting colors in a jar, or mix them up in a plastic bag, and include the recipe on a card.

¼ cup each: red kidney beans, green split peas, yellow split peas, lentils, black-eyed peas, navy beans, pinto beans, rinsed and picked over

2 tablespoons fine pearl barley

1 bay leaf

1 teaspoon garlic powder

1 tablespoon chili powder

½ teaspoon dried thyme leaves

1 teaspoon dried savory

1 beef or ham bone

2 quarts water

1 can (28 ounces) tomatoes, mashed

2 tablespoons fresh or bottled lemon juice

1. Place the beans in a 2-cup container and package the herbs in a separate smaller container. Store in a cool, dark place away from heat and light.

2. To prepare, mix the beans in a large pot or bowl and cover with water. Soak the beans overnight. Pour off the water.

3. In a large soup pot, combine the beans with the barley, spices, bone, water, and tomatoes. Simmer 2½ – 3 hours in a covered pot, until the beans are tender.

4. Add the lemon juice and cook another 15 minutes. Remove the bone.

SPLIT PEA SOUP

1 pound (about 2¼ cups) dried green split peas, rinsed and picked over

6 cups chicken or vegetable stock

2 tablespoons butter

½ teaspoon salt

1	medium onion, chopped
1	celery stalk, chopped with leaves
1	clove garlic, minced
2	medium carrots, chopped
1	medium potato, cubed
1	cup diced ham or turkey sausage, cooked (optional)

1. Combine all the ingredients except the ham in a heavy 6-quart saucepan.

2. Bring to a boil, covered, then reduce the heat and simmer for 2½ hours. A slow cooker may be used on low for 6–8 hours. Stir occasionally.

3. The meat can be added the last 5 minutes to heat through.

SHIITAKE MUSHROOM SOUP

Never underestimate the potency of dried shiitake mushrooms. This richly flavored soup will be one of your most memorable.

3	ounces dried shiitake mushrooms
1	medium potato, unpeeled
1½	quarts chicken broth
2	tablespoons butter
2	bunches scallions, coarsely chopped, including tops
4	tablespoons frozen apple juice concentrate
½	teaspoon salt
⅛	teaspoon freshly ground black pepper
1	cup half-and-half

1. Reconstitute the mushrooms by pouring boiling water over them to cover. Let stand 30 minutes.

2. Drain the mushrooms on paper towels, reserving the liquid for added flavor in other soups and sauces.

3. Wash the potato and cut into ½-inch cubes.

4. Heat the broth to a simmer in a 4-quart pot. Add the cubed potato and cook until tender, 10 minutes.

5. Sauté the mushrooms in butter along with the scallions in a large skillet, until the scallions are soft. Add the mushroom mixture to the simmering stock. Increase the heat to medium high and cook for 15 minutes.

6. Stir in the juice concentrate, salt, and pepper. Spoon out the solids and puree them in a blender or food processor.

7. Return the puree to the pot, stir in the half-and-half, and reheat slightly. Serve immediately.

MUSHROOM-BARLEY SOUP

This great recipe answers the question, "What on earth can I have for Saturday lunch?"

½	cup dried medium-size barley
¼	cup dried mushroom slices of your choice
2	tablespoons dried minced onions
2	tablespoons dried parsley
2	tablespoons dried thyme
2	bay leaves
2	chicken (or vegetable) bouillon cubes

1. Combine all the ingredients in a clean 1-pint canning jar. Store in a dark, dry place until needed.

2. Make the soup by adding the dried ingredients to 1 quart of boiling water in a 2-quart saucepan.

3. Cover, reduce the heat, and simmer until the barley and mushrooms are tender, about 45 minutes.

VEGETABLE RICE BEEF SOUP

This is a great way to use those dried vegetables. The ones listed are just suggestions — use them or any combination from your stock of dried goods.

2	cups dried vegetables:
½	cup chopped onions
½	cup chopped green beans
1	cup chopped carrots
2	cups boiling water
1	large, meaty, beef soup bone
6	cups water or beef broth
1½	cups tomato puree, or sauce, or chopped whole tomatoes
1	clove garlic, minced
½	teaspoon salt
2	tablespoons dried parsley
1	bay leaf

¼   teaspoon freshly ground black pepper
¼   cup uncooked long-grain white rice

1. Rehydrate the vegetables in 2 cups of boiling water for 1–2 hours.

2. In a heavy soup pot, cover the bone with 6 cups of water or broth and simmer, covered, for 1 hour. Remove the bone and reserve.

3. Add the tomatoes, garlic, and seasonings. Add the rice to the broth. Simmer, covered, for 20-30 minutes.

4. Cut the meat from the bone; add the meat to the pot.

5. Add the rehydrated vegetables and simmer, covered, for 45–60 minutes.

HERBED RICE MIX

Your dried herbs keep on giving in this blend. Pour this mix in a handsome, reclaimed jar, add a bow of raffia or ribbon, and plain rice becomes a festive gift.

Mix

1   cup long-grain converted white rice, uncooked
2   beef bouillon cubes or 2 all-natural vegetable bouillon cubes
¼   teaspoon salt
½   teaspoon dried marjoram
½   teaspoon dried thyme
1   teaspoon dried chives

To cook

2   cups water
1   tablespoon butter or oil

1. Combine the ingredients for the mix and store them in an airtight container away from heat and light.

2. To cook, combine the mixture with the water in a heavy saucepan about 1 quart in size. Add 1 tablespoon of butter. Bring to a boil and cover. Turn the heat to medium, and do not lift the lid. Simmer the rice exactly 30 minutes.

3. Leaving the lid snugly in place, turn off the heat and let the rice rest for 30 minutes. Uncover and fluff the rice with a fork. Serve immediately.

4. Leftovers can be frozen for later use.

DRIED-MUSHROOM RAGOUT

Your dried mushrooms contribute concentrated flavor year-round. This recipe will make a Sunday-night supper a real treat.

1   cup boiling water
1   cup dried mushrooms of your choice
2   tablespoons butter or margarine
2   tablespoons all-purpose flour
1   cup milk
½   teaspoon salt
⅛   teaspoon white pepper
¼   cup Parmesan cheese

1. Combine the water and mushrooms in a 1-quart saucepan. Simmer, covered, 20–30 minutes or until mushrooms are completely reconstituted.

2. Drain, reserving the liquid for other uses; such as soups.

3. Preheat the oven to 350°F.

4. Melt the butter in a 1-quart flame-proof casserole. Stir in the flour and gradually add the milk. Stir constantly, until the white sauce is smooth and thick. Add the mushrooms and seasonings. Top with the cheese.

5. Bake for 25–35 minutes.

6. Serve over toast triangles.

MEXICAN SALAD *TERRA NOBLE*

Dried banana chips lend a tropical note to this cool, satisfying salad.

2–3   medium carrots, shredded (1½ cups)
2   cups shredded red cabbage
2   cucumbers, cleaned and diced
1   tablespoon sesame seeds, toasted
1   large head shredded iceberg lettuce (4 cups)
½   cups chopped dry-roasted, salted peanuts
1   cup dried banana chips
1   fresh pear, diced

Dressing

⅔   cup olive oil
¼   cup lime juice, freshly squeezed (2 medium limes)

1. In a large salad bowl, combine all salad ingredients and toss well.

2. In a small bowl, combine the oil and lime juice and mix until smooth.

3. Add dressing, ¼ cup at a time, until salad fixings are coated according to taste.

TOMATO LEATHER

This is one vegetable leather definitely worth trying.

4–5 medium tomatoes, chopped (2 cups)
1   medium onion, chopped
½   large stalk celery, chopped (¼ cup)
½   teaspoon salt
¼   teaspoon freshly ground black pepper

1. Mix all the ingredients in a 2-quart saucepan and simmer, covered, for 15 minutes.

2. Cool slightly and puree in a food processor. (Drape a wet cloth over the lid to prevent hot liquid from splattering out of the bowl.)

3. Return the puree to the pan and cook another 15 minutes, until thickened. Stir frequently and toward the end constantly to prevent burning the puree.

4. Spread the mixture on a cookie sheet covered in plastic wrap and tilt the sheet until the puree is evenly distributed.

5. Dry the leather in a 120°F oven for 6–8 hours, until the mixture can be pulled away from the plastic wrap easily.

6. Invert the leather on another plastic wrap sheet (and remove the bottom plastic sheet, which is now on the top). Let it dry in the 120°F oven for about 6 more hours.

7. Remove the wrap and let it cool to room temperature.

8. Wrap the leather carefully in aluminum foil or plastic wrap. Roll and store it in an airtight container away from light and heat for up to 1 year. (Some people prefer dusting the roll with cornstarch to keep it from sticking before rolling and storing.) To use, cut off portions from the roll for a nutritious snack.

BARBECUED BEEF JERKY

This is adapted from the recipe for Barbecued Beef Jerky in the Ball Blue Book. *Once you've tasted homemade jerky, you'll never want the store-bought variety again.*

3	pounds lean beef (flank or round), trimmed of all fat
1	cup ketchup
½	cup red wine vinegar
¼	cup brown sugar
2	tablespoons Worcestershire sauce
2	teaspoons dry mustard
1	teaspoon onion powder
1	teaspoon salt
¼	teaspoon cracked black pepper

1. For ease in cutting, freeze beef, uncovered, in a bowl until ice crystals form, 1–2 hours. Cut into thin strips against the grain (an electric knife is good for this).

2. Combine the remaining ingredients in a large nonporous bowl. Add the beef strips, cover the bowl tightly, and refrigerate overnight.

3. To dry the beef strips using a dehydrator, follow manufacturer's directions.

4. To use your own oven for drying jerky, set the temperature at 145°F.

5. Drain the meat and pat it dry. Lay the meat strips on oven racks and prop the oven door open with a wooden spoon handle to allow the moisture to escape. Dry the meat 4–6 hours, then let it cool. Test one piece by bending. If moisture is present, dry a little longer. If it does not break, it's ready (if it does, it is overcooked).

6. Place the dried meat in a freezer container and freeze 3 days.

7. Store the jerky in an airtight container in a dry, cool place for 3 weeks, or 2 months in your refrigerator, or up to 6 months in the freezer.

ORIENTAL TURKEY JERKY

Low fat and delicious, this turkey jerky will spice up your next picnic.

1	pound boned, skinned turkey breast, trimmed of all fat
¼	teaspoon onion powder
¼	teaspoon garlic

½   cup water

¼   cup soy sauce

2   teaspoons Worcestershire sauce

2   tablespoons firmly packed brown sugar

1   teaspoon freshly ground black pepper

1. To tenderize the meat, pound the turkey breast between layers of waxed paper. For ease in slicing, freeze it until ice crystals form, and then slice thinly against the grain (an electric knife is good for this).

2. Combine the remaining ingredients in a nonporous bowl, stirring well. Add the turkey breast slices and refrigerate overnight, tightly covered.

3. To dry using a dehydrator, follow manufacturer's directions.

4. To use the oven, preheat the oven to 150°F.

5. Place the drained, patted-dry meat strips on the oven racks. Prop open the oven door with a wooden spoon handle to allow moisture to escape. Dry the meat 18–24 hours. Test one piece by letting it cool. Bend it. If moisture is present, dry the meat a little longer. If it doesn't break, it is ready. (If it does break, it's overdone.)

6. Place the meat in a clean freezer container and freeze 3 days.

7. Store it in an airtight container in a dry, cool, place for 3 weeks, or 2 months in the refrigerator, or up to 6 months in the freezer.

CRANBERRY BREAD

Dried cranberries are a good addition to muffins, waffles, and cookies — delicious!

¾   cup orange juice

1   cup dried cranberries with sweetener added

1   cup whole-wheat flour

1   cup all-purpose flour

½   cup wheat germ

¼   teaspoon salt

2   teaspoons baking powder

½   teaspoon baking soda

Rind of 1 orange, grated

¾   cup honey

1   egg

2   tablespoons oil

1. In a small saucepan, heat the orange juice just to boiling. Add the dried cranberries and let them sit for 30 minutes, until reconstituted.

2. Grease a loaf pan and line it with waxed paper. Grease the waxed paper.

3. Combine the dry ingredients in a separate 4-cup bowl.

4. Preheat the oven to 350°F. Mix together the orange rind, honey, egg, and oil. Add the reconstituted cranberries with any remaining juices and mix well.

5. Add the dry ingredients gradually to the cranberry mix, stirring after each addition. Stir until smooth, but do not overmix.

6. Pour the batter into a prepared loaf pan and bake for 50 minutes, or until a toothpick inserted in the center comes out clean. Cool the bread for 15 minutes in the pan, then turn out the bread onto a cake rack to cool completely.

APPLE COFFEE CAKE

Dried apples make this a great winter treat. Double this recipe, if you want to save one for later. These may be frozen.

2	cups dried apples
1	teaspoon lemon juice
½	cup butter or margarine
¼	cup sugar
2	eggs
1½	cups all-purpose flour
½	teaspoon salt
2	teaspoons baking powder
½	cup milk
1	teaspoon vanilla extract

Sugar topping

½	cup sugar
2	teaspoons ground cinnamon

1. Grease and flour a 9-inch square pan or glass casserole.

2. In a nonreactive saucepan, combine apples, lemon juice, and enough boiling water to cover. Cook until fruit is reconstituted. Drain.

3. Preheat the oven to 325°F.

4. Cream the butter and sugar until smooth. Add the eggs, one at a time, beating well after each addition.

5. In a separate bowl, sift the dry ingredients. Add the dry ingredients, alternately with the milk, to the cream mixture. Add the vanilla and beat well.

6. Pour the batter into the pan and top with the rehydrated apples. Mix the sugar and cinnamon and sprinkle on top.

7. Bake at 325°F for 30–45 minutes, or until a toothpick inserted in the center comes out clean.

QUIET SPIRIT TEA BLEND

This tea has a wonderful calming effect on nerves and the digestive tract.

½   **cup dried rosemary leaves**
½   **cup dried lavender flowers**
½   **cup dried mint leaves**
¼   **cup chamomile**
¼   **cup dried cloves**

1. Combine all the ingredients and store in an airtight container away from the heat and light.

2. Use 1 teaspoon of mix to 6 ounces of boiling water, using a tea ball or a teapot with a strainer. Let it steep 5–8 minutes. Delicious hot or cold.

HIGH-CALCIUM TONIC

A great morning ritual or afternoon tea break, this concoction has more calcium than other herb teas thanks to the chamomile and oat straw.

2   **ounces (3 tablespoons) dried oat straw**
2   **ounces (4 tablespoons) dried chamomile flowers**
1   **ounce (3 tablespoons) dried alfalfa**
1   **ounce (3 tablespoons) dried red raspberry leaves**
2   **ounces (3 tablespoons) dried mint leaves**

1. Mix all the ingredients and store them in an airtight container in a cool, dark place.

2. To brew, use 1 teaspoon per 6 ounces of boiling water. Infuse 10 minutes. Use a tea ball or strain from the pot.

Keep Your Pantry Well Stocked with More Books from Storey

The Backyard Homestead Book of Kitchen Know-How
by Andrea Chesman

Get the most from your homegrown foods with this friendly and comprehensive guide to gathering, preserving, and eating the fruits of your labor. You'll learn how to can fresh produce, mill flour, render lard, make butter and cheese, and much more!

The Beginner's Guide to Making and Using Dried Foods by Teresa Marrone

From apples to watermelon, asparagus to zucchini, basil to beef, you'll find detailed instructions for drying with a dehydrator, an oven, or the sun. And more than 140 recipes help you use your dried foods in a range of delicious dishes.

Fermented Vegetables
by Kirsten K. Shockey & Christopher Shockey

Get to work making your own kimchi, pickles, sauerkraut, and more with this colorful and delicious guide. Beautiful photography illustrates methods to ferment 64 vegetables and herbs, along with dozens of creative recipes.

Preserving Wild Foods
by Matthew Weingarten & Raquel Pelzel

Forage wild ingredients from the sea, forests, and rivers, and preserve them for your own kitchen using old-world methods. Dozens of delicious recipes teach you how to cure, can, smoke, and pickle your foraged bounty.

Put 'em Up!
by Sherri Brooks Vinton

This comprehensive guide to preserving gives you bright flavors, flexible batch sizes, and modern methods. The simple instructions and more than 150 delicious recipes cover freezing, drying, canning, and pickling.

Join the conversation. Share your experience with this book, learn more about Storey Publishing's authors, and read original essays and book excerpts at storey.com. Look for our books wherever quality books are sold or call 800-441-5700.